To walk within a dream

**Roy Randolph Andrews
AKA (The hot shot poet)**

To walk within a dream

Roy Randolph Andrews AKA (The hot shot poet)

ISBN:1518717969
ISBN-13:9781518717963

DEDICATION

I would like to Thank Createspace.com for making my books possible.
They truly stand by their customers at all times.

I also want to thank my many friends & family that have all stood by me as I attempt to make my dreams a perfect Reality.
(all my love to you all)

Susan Mary Andrews=my wife

Austin Roy Andrews=my youngest son

Stephen Randolph Andrews=my oldest Brother

Johnny Terrill Andrews=my second too the oldest brother

Chuck & Georgia Russo=my brother-n-law & sister –n-law for their honest Inspiration through all my work.

Christa Kelley=one of my new family members Who seem to be Reading & liking my poems

Also Serena Ashley=another of my new family

members for taking the time to see what I write,
Greg & Holly Conti=my sister & Brother –n-law

Cindy Royale=my youngest sister
Janice Moore=my mother

Jason Anthony Andrews=my oldest son

(My daughters)
Jennifer Marione Lancaster

Amanda Lynn Andrews

Julie Ann Andrews

Aron Leigh Andrews

Ariel Leann Andrews

Even though some have gotten married & their last
name has changed but they will always be an
Andrews to me
Also the many family members from all parts of the
country
For simply noticing the work I do & knowing
It runs in the family,
For always overlooking my many faults & excepting
me as I am

ACKNOWLEDGMENTS

To all the people who have taken a place in my
life & making all I do possible today,
(THANK YOU)

The only way I know to express my gratitude

To the many people that have stood by me
while I expressed my hunger to follow my
dream is to simply (continue writing)

I do hope all who read my work

Can see what I mean when I say

If you want to know about me,
It is simple
(Read my work)

I am
Roy Randolph Andrews
AKA
The Hot Shot Poet

& this
Is my Legacy

To follow a dream is to live that dream,
If you can only believe with all your heart
(Anything is possible)

A beautiful Day

I wake up every morning
with a smile on my face
for I know I am blessed
with this simple little place

it holds so many memories
time can't take away
memories I'll keep alive
until my dying day

my homes not great to look at
it was not made for show
it was built as a special place
to watch my family grow

to me this is stable
as a person could ever be
I don't worry about tomorrow
when it happens we will see

so this home is a castle
for my children & my wife
a place that I belong
& will throughout my life

A fear in life

(hold on to your life as if today was your last
day on earth)

driving down the highway
all legal & is right
within the blink of an eye
my day had turned to night

no doubt I saw it coming
with a sixteen-foot trailer full of weight
I tried hard to divert the accident
but it was much too late

a seventeen-year-old boy
although driving all alone
he had run straight through the red-light
while texting on a phone

by the time I got my truck stopped
jackknifed & in a ditch
I jumped out & Ran to the young boy
& saw how my life had switched

he was scared but alright
& I could feel no pain
the fear had taken over me
& suddenly it drained

once I knew he was alright
it felt like something with my sight
I was unconscious on the highway
my day had turned to night

I guess the statement that I'm making
or at least trying hard to say
live life at its fullest
you may not have another day

In memory of Edna May Johnson

for 1 simple woman
being strong everyday
but all she ever wanted
was for the pain to go away

she thought she hid it well
but all could plainly see
this is what she wanted
her private destiny

to be back with her husband
a love so pure & true
giving all their heart to family
doing all they had to do

no more pain & misery
at peace with in herself
any grudges or hard feelings
she put them on a shelf

Edna Johnson has now passed away
& although it's very sad
I see the smile that's on her face
she's gone to be with dad

I wrote this for a very dear woman she was my

mother-n-law for many years & always treated
me like family
I love you mom & in my heart now you can
finally smile,
for today you finally get to sit in heaven next to
your husband
& we all know you wanted this most of all.

you will always be in

our hearts,

love always
Roy Randolph Andrews

&
Austin Roy Andrews

To walk within a dream

A prayer answered

as my world grows stronger
in every single part
this life that I live
is so precious to my heart

the simple words I love you
are precious words to hear
when they are spoken by my son
my destination is clear

our new life together
is beyond a dream come true
he's the best friend I could have
in everything I do

he is my perfect angel
my inspiration everyday
with the little things he does
and the words that he would say

as grateful and as thankful
as a dad could ever be
God knew just what I was needing
when he gave my son to me

ACCOMPLISHMENTS

my words are my accomplishments
in this life I lead
they give me strength to carry on
with all the hope I need

my hopes and dreams are simple
I hope that all can see
how a precious little smile
can mean the world to me

I do not ask for much in life
I do what must be done
waiting to be excepted
me and my son

for anyone to understand us
the very true insight
learn to read between the lines
in the poetry I write

this is truly me
I think my words will show it
I welcome you to my little world
I'm the Hot Shot Poet

Aiming for the heart

will she ever realize
that we were meant to be
or are we really over
is she through with me

I thought we'd always be together
right from the very start
I never thought that someone else
would ever take your heart

well I got overconfident
that much I can see
she gave my world to another
it was meant to be

she is looking for something
I don't think she will find
someone who truly understands her
not playing with her mind

a man will tell her anything
to get where he wants to be
sometimes our worst lessons
are our own reality

I have to let this go
& everybody knows it
she is aiming for the heart
of the hot shot poet

all my pride

your hair your lips
your shape your size
your all I see
through these eyes'

your gentle touch
your warm caress
to me you are
the very best

I have no shame
nothing to hide
you are my world
you are my pride

the prettiest woman
ever in my life
I'm so proud to say
that she is my wife

I hope she's growing
tired of that place
maybe she will come home
& share this space

I watch through the clouds
to the heavens above
just waiting to hold
my only true love

alone in the dark

as I sit here & watch
the break of day
as the tranquility of night
just fades away

I hear a bird chirping
in the trees so dark
I don't have a dog
but I hear one bark

I walk in my yard
just to see
it's not my dog
but he's barking at me

he shows me his teeth
& hair stood up on his back
but when I ran at him
I think he lost track

now all I see
is him from behind
no doubt he thinks
I've lost my mind

as he Runs like crazy
crashes into a tree
he was trying his best
to get away from me

I have no fear
of a dog or a bark
or what creep's around
in the midst of the dark

I'm not sure what makes me
React this way
it's always been me
what more can I say

this is my choice
the life I live
I give my all
& too all I give

I've been told I'm crazy
& this may be true
but this is me
doing just what I do

I have no fear
or no Reason to hide
some call it crazy
but I call it pride

all I know
is it's easy to see
it's the Andrews spirit
that lives in me

emotion's & tempers
balled up into one
that's all I can say
except this poem is done

appearance

I look at life as carpentry
like the building of a shelf
we get caught in the design
& we forget about our self

the measurements are right
the looks are all in place
but something is still missing
in a single empty space

we go back & recalibrate
all that we have done
looking for a single flaw
but the appearance shows us none

although appearance means a lot
it is not everything
it's the heart within the structure
& the happiness it brings

it also must be sturdy
built to take a load
like a heart with a destination
all alone out on the road

every piece has a certain place
& only there is where it fits
like words never spoken
to a heart that called it quits

Austin Roy Andrews (Buckaroo)

losing you was hard
what a perfect way to start
a better way of life
but not without my heart

I'm looking for my sanity
in everything I do
all my inspiration
is looking for me too

he calls me everyday
because he really needs to know
that his daddy loves him very much
my hopes are that it shows

there's nothing that could change that
in any kind of way
I need to show my love for him
every single day

to see his precious smile
sparkly eye's & glowing face
he makes me feel so needed
& nothing can replace

just in case you see this
smile real big for me
you are your daddy's buckaroo
& you will always be

everything will be alright
you will know it then
we will be back together
& our new life will begin

believing is a must

I did something different
in a much inspiring way
I dropped down on my knees
& I talked to God today

I had a voice come to me
saying don't be sad
the hurting deep inside of you
kept you angry & so mad

he said he has watched over me
everywhere I'd go
although I didn't realize
the pain would surely show

he said I hid behind a smile
that all could surely see
but he said he always knew
what was hurting me

all the answers to my prayers
were easy to retrieve
he said all I had to do
was truly believe

he knew I did believe in him
but for so long I left him out
for he cannot show the way
if the heart has any doubt

if my life wants to see
what dreams are all made of
I must know I can't have happiness
without our God above

can't stop missing

(trying hard is never enough)

glassy eye's & memories
are all I seem to find
every day that I wake up
it's all that's on my mind

they haunt my mind constantly
no matter what I do
as long as I am thinking
I'm always being blue

a little boy who needs me
though we are far apart
he is everything I hurt for
he truly is my heart

nothing seems to matter
but to simply find a way
I miss him every second
of every single day

there are forces on this earth
stronger than the eyes can see
I'm praying that they help to
bring my baby back to me

the hardest thing I've ever done
is lose that precious little touch
of the child that's so much of me
I truly love so much

Christmas

a day meant to be happy
no matter what you see
I miss having all my kids
all surrounding me

but all will be okay
this much I think is true
I believe I am in their thoughts
no matter what they do

just look up towards the heavens
to the star that shines so bright
& know that I'm also looking at
this star with you tonight

I hope your lives are what you hoped for
as you fallow all your dreams
I'm sorry it took me so long
to know just what that means

just know your always thought about
no matter what you do
I love you very much
& merry Christmas to you

Devotion of a Dad

I've tried so hard to avoid this
not knowing what to do
I didn't want this to happen
to me or to you

but things have changed dramatically
they cannot be undone
this is about happiness
the happiness of our son

you tell him he will see me soon
to keep his mind contained
we both know it's a lie
& so the fact Remains

we cannot both be with him
you've made it very clear
now I will do what I must
for the child I love so dear

if you've never read between the lines
I would assume that you will start
you've tried so hard to destroy me
& tear my world apart

I've tried so hard to make this right
now I will show you how
you really are not ready
for what is coming now

legal Retribution
I'm fighting for my son
we will see who has this victory
when your divorce is done

I am truly sorry for this
& what I have to do
but our son needs his father
more than I need you

Do you see me? (as I am)

do you see me
as I truly am
or am I an image
you can't bring back again

that image you are wanting
I can never be
because in this world I'm simply meant
to be no one but me

your attention I was bound for
long before you knew
just doing what I'm good at
and doing what I do

so if you get past this
the crush no one can see
I hope you will be honored
to know someone like me

I am not worthy of a crush
or things that come within
but this is where true life
always begins

so simply put, you see me
do you see what I do?
do you know who I'm writing for
is no one else but you?

Doctors

I won't go to the Doctor
because something always clicks
they always ask what's going on
when obviously your sick

if we knew that answer
maybe we would know what to do
it would make life simpler
for me & you

I'm still thankful for Doctors
& the service they provide
they keep our hearts working
& our eye's opened wide

a simple little thank you
would have probably been just fine
but everyone has their opinion
& this is just mine

Endangerment

I deal with my problems
as they come at will
but today what I encountered
made my world stand still

the x-wife had visitation
against everything I feared
I let her take them from my sight
& now she's disappeared

how could I not have seen this
it's her ammo in her games
all charges have been filed
& she has herself to blame

this time I will not back off
my children are my life
I want the legal prosecution
of only my x-wife

if she wanted to hurt someone
she should come after me
no one should ever mess with
a man's own destiny

she has truly underestimated
what my dreams are all made of
my children are my everything
my life time full of love

I feel they are in danger
with only so much I can do
so if my ex wants to know what's happening
the law is coming after you

Families happy life

this is where reality
kicks me in the face
her heart has found a new love
nowhere near this place

I feel their hearts are happy
I think everyone can see
he now holds the angel
I thought was meant for me

so much for raising family
together as one
for now, he has them all
my dreams are done

I got just what I asked for
but didn't pass the test
so have a very merry Christmas
& I wish you all the best

Fix It

find out what it is
whatever you must do
there must be a reason
she no longer believes in you

if you have never cheated
& you never once told her a lie
then get down to the confusing part
of finding out why

chances are that the answer
is something you do not want to hear
it could possibly destroy
something you hold very dear

none the less it's the truth
you must seek to find
where you are not so confused
or walking around blind

keep in mind the truth can hurt you
but the cold reality
is this is part of life
& what must be will be

the not knowing is the hardest part
that you will ever face
but you must find out if you can
to put respective back in its place

so serious or silly
you must give your heart a rest
so when you find your answer
I wish you all the best

Gator bait

tonight I hunted gators
just a Bouie knife & me
to see if I'm still swamp Rat
what growing up would be

Raised in the everglades
we only fished for one thing
only what was dangerous
there was no in between

at dark I would jump in
just to see what we could see
to see what all would show up
coming after me

you would be surprised
red eye's everywhere
guns aimed at all the eye's
my friends were all there

shots being fired from everywhere
not one eye was ever missed
the men they felt me blessed
with the most of nature's kiss

today I find it funny
I've went from gator bait
to writing real life poetry
that's worthy of debate

yes, I'm southern country
right down to the core
& as I live & breath
I am forever more

Get it right

if I was given one more chance
to spend my life with you
I thought that you should know
just what I want to do

I'll spend every waking moment
showing you who I adore
& I want to hold you close to me
always & forever more

I want to hold your hand
where ever we might be
I want to show the world
that you're a part of me

All the little things
that we never did before
I want to do them all
for now, & ever more

precious there is no doubt
the things I didn't do
but now I want to make it right
for me & for you

GONE

I finally got away
from the Baker county jail
I tried to stay so silent
with so very much to tell

now I'm back at Coleman
penitentiary
it's really not all bad
it's what you make it out to be

when you have to do time
not wanting it to last
in a federal prison
it moves pretty fast

but don't get the wrong impression
you're paying for a crime
that apparently you committed
now you have to do the time

will you take this as a lesson
will you learn from it
will you make the same mistakes
or will you finally quit

good morning

good morning to all
it is a beautiful day
the sun is out, no clouds to see
I like it just that way

my kids are all dressed & gone to school
no bad moods that I could see
it makes my day when they're that way
at least it does to me

I will start back today with my older poems
I just have so many to share
I love the responses that I get
it shows people still do care

no doubt it's what I know
the second thing I do best
Raising my kids is number one
for that there is no test

I have four of my girls on here now
in my footsteps they follow close
they write what they are feeling
& that's what means the most

so if you find a poem that belongs to me
insulting in any way
I will remove it so very fast
because that is just my way

I tend to stay away from
offensive poetry with everything I write
I'd see laughter & smiles any day
or try with all my might

Gotta-Get-R-Done

the handyman service
that for years I learned to Run
has a difference to its name
it's Gotta-Get-R-Done

it specifies completely
the job I have to do
with Respect to the costumer
& the job I have to do

in 1990
my business started with this name
now up to this day
it has always been the same

satisfaction is my goal
the most important guarantee
just show me what the job is
& leave the Rest to me

costumers always happy
complaints, there are none
I am the man behind the name
Gotta-Get-R-Done

HAPPY BIRTHDAY

happy birthday to my little prince
he's finally turning ten
I hold these precious moments
knowing they won't come back again

our road so full of obstacles
sometimes we didn't know what to say
but as our bloodline teaches us
nothing gets in our way

thanks to the grace of god
your healthy & your strong
I see so much of me in you
that's why we get along

through trials & tribulations
just doing what we do
I love you more than life itself
you are my dream come true

so Austin Roy Andrews
I hope my words will show
you're my Inspiration
and I hope you always know

Have faith in You

they say if you Really love something
you have to let it go
if it comes back it's yours
but sometimes you never know

our hearts want to believe
that our loved ones will come home
as our tears come down like Rain
from feeling so alone

we feel as if we've lost it all
like our worlds come to an end
when all we Really needed
for our broken heart's to mend

was simply to have faith
in the plan God's made for us
even if you don't believe
sometimes you have to trust

in something you can't see
we're always told he's there
he could be right there beside you
anytime & anywhere

now holier than thou
so many claim to be
but they are no better than us
in all Reality

they feel that they will go to heaven
& I say let them go
because if this is the truth
well we may never know

they say they fallow gods plan
the so called guiding light
but it's hard to find a path
to a plan that is so bright

I do believe he made us
& put us on this earth
to live our lives & prosper
& mommies to give birth

so I say that I believe
in heaven & of hell
but there both Right here on earth
as far as I can tell

having hope

picturing the past
when you use to hold me tight
no matter what confused me
you'd always make it right

it seemed no matter what
if our hearts were in despair
with your soft words & your touch
you would easily make repairs

I truly miss the feeling
when I would look into your eye's
no matter what was wrong
your love would hypnotize

I thought it was impossible
to love anyone this way
I wish that you were here with me
I'm praying everyday

I never could replace you
or the feeling of your touch
so I'm hoping that you need me to
& I love you very much

He knows

they say if you believe in him
& believe with all your might
even your darkest day
will always shine bright

we have all been through our hard times
they become Reality
it's hard to except
but what will be will be

this world holds no favorites
this much I know is true
so be it wrong or right
I'll keep doing what I do

no doubt I'm far from perfect
with no perfect words to say
but as long as I believe in him
all will be okay

he knows that I believe in him
I'm sure no one can see
he's the only one who knows
why I'm busy being me

Heartbreaker

I use to have a Hobby
I was so wild & free
I would break a lady's heart
so everyone could see

it didn't seem to matter
for no reason did I care
all that I would think
was pretty girls beware

I didn't have a problem
I attracted them with ease
I'd speak what they wish to hear
anything they please

I never did consider
or even try to see
The pain I was inflicting
until it was done to me

but only one female in my life
could ever touch my pride
or make me pour out
the way I feel inside

now I look back
at all the broken hearts
& wish that I could take back
what I tore apart

well that was my wilder days
I seem to have no fear
now all that I inflict
is happiness & cheer

I can't help you

there is nothing I can do
to change the way, you are
the way you've made your life to be
has changed a scratch into a scar

I have known you all your life
but I can't defend what I don't know
you have chosen the path your walking down
not knowing where you'll go

you have chosen all the wrong things
in the life you choose to live
your giving what you call happiness
but you have none to give

it seems what you call happiness
is your nose stuck to a pill
well can't never could until he tried
& you probably never will

I'm ashamed of what I've found out
& I have no doubt it's true
I hope that you will seek some help
before it destroys you

I have written you this poem
to try to say to you goodbye
I will not stay in your life
& simply watch you die

so just look in your mirror
& reflect on what you see
what you're looking at is sad
a self-inflicted tragedy

I really think he knows

how far can we bend
until we have to break
when all of our emotions
have all they can take

wrapping up my heart
& tying it so tight
while giving it my everything
to try & do it right

to try to stop the loneliness
that's taken hold of me
& for my little boy
being all that I can be

never any doubts
if his father loves him so
the one thing I am sure of
that he will always know

he simply is my everything
that life is all made of
this is my reaction
& for sure this Fathers love

I'm to blame

the hardest thing
that I can do
is to look around
& not see you

I blame myself
I really do
for forgetting to show
how much I love you

I wish I had seen it
before it was too late
before the love you had
had turned to hate

it is my fault
& I'm sorry for this
I didn't know I would hurt
when you were missed

so no matter where you go
& no matter what you do
there's a special place inside of me
that belongs to you

Image

life is not always
the good things that we see
but still we don't dispute
what will be, will be

we paint a pretty picture
hoping everyone will think
life is not impossible
& won't change within a blink

when I look beyond the image
of the man I am today
I'm thankful for my courage
& the ability to say

I'm proud of who I am
my flaws belong to me
the image in my mirror
I hope is all you see

but in case you can see
beyond the shadow of the doubt
then chances are you understand
what life is all about

the sun

the sun took a break
to chat with the moon
when he saw he was running late
he said I must leave soon

there are those plants & people
that all depend on me
I somehow make the gardens grow
& bring the light so all can see

there isn't any time
my job is never old
I bring a smile to many faces
& make the warmth when they are cold

& the early morning fog
puts limits on their sight
they depend on me to dry it up
& make everything so bright

so every single day
I show pride & dignity
because I know a lot that happens
does depend on me

inbox

if you want to cry your heart out
I'm sure you'll find a way
it just might be in memories
or words that people say

it might be in an inbox
with a simple little look
you will see what you have
with your page you call Facebook

simple little treasures
that no one seems to see
they open up a verse
to a common destiny

it will either make you smile
or bring you straight to tears
bring you fields of joy
or make you face your fears

either way I've been there
I've seen which way to go
now if you'll ever feel it
only you will know

Inspiration for the Poet

Two precious little ladies
they love me all to pieces
these precious little ladies
they are my nieces

I had forgotten who I am
it didn't matter anymore
I did my life a favor
closing hearts door

they seem to have come from nowhere
straight into my life
as my heart was being broken
by the one I called my wife

they seem to stay so close to me
never straying very far
they hold the name of Andrews
& proud of who they are

I am Honored to be a part of this
I hope that all can see
I am Roy Randolph Andrews
& I will always be

Instructions

we write titles
to fit books
we gave our all
& all it took

to assure that our title
did not go a stray
that it blended in
in every way

we don't compromise
the story inside
but we let it all out
with nothing to hide

to show what we feel
this is our way
to tell the world
what we have to say

line to line
our story unfolds
it comes to life
as the words are told

each little word
on each little line
describing something
of a place or time

each paragraph
that you will see
is created from life
to be the best it can be

from beginning to end
& in every way
our story must carry
what we have to say

to break a heart
or to help one mend
the life of a poet
from beginning to end

just a dad

exercising my beliefs
and the dreams I once had
trying to be responsible
through being just a dad

everybody gives suggestions
but nobody seems to see
no one can ever be this dad
unless you can be me

I hear what families go through
their ups & downs in life
but everything they throw at me
somebody has a wife

well there is no wife here
which shows I'm not like you
I must be at my best
just doing what I do

no doubt this life confuses me
& most would see it bad
but I write this poem in confidence
no doubt I'm just a dad

just dad

the temper just goes crazy
so deep through my soul
it seems my son is the only one
that grips what makes me whole

I tend to scare myself
when control is not insight
but with my son beside me
I try with all my might

he seems to know what sets me off
and the message it will bring
he knows just what will happen
not an ordinary thing

one man crossed the line
made a threat to my son
now he knows that this dad
will do what must be done

I did not mean to hurt him
I gave it all I had
but coming from the heart of me
I am just a dad

Learning from mistakes

(the learning curve for sure)

for so many years I've hidden
deep inside a shell
staying bottled up inside
thinking I was doing well

I watched my world fall apart
Right before my eye's
I had to hit Rock bottom
before I would Realize

I was going through the motions
just trying to play the part
just doing what I had to
to protect my heart

life has many obstacles
new one's every day
the hardest one I've ever faced
was when my world had walked away

my downfall was my thinking
it won't happen to me
now I spend my days alone
with this cold Reality

the point that I'm putting out
is no matter what you do
if you think that it cannot
it can happen to you

so hold your true love closely
show their special in every way
your love will stand the test of time
growing stronger every day

Lies

something so addictive
I cannot tell you why
it starts out small & grows
this thing is called a lie

they always start out small
& then they seem to grow
they never seem to stop
this is how I know

I'm fed up with the people
who do it & don't know why
they don't know how to function
unless they get to lie

they can't see the addiction
but to me it's very clear
they do not care how it hurts
they simply have no fear

so if you get caught up
in this mixed up little way
be prepared to face reality
it will catch up to you one day

life will change

my life will change
for all to see
if I am what you're looking for
you'll have to find me

I've chased these crazy dreams
& always done my best
but when the sad outweighs the happy
my heart needs a rest

the only smiles left in me
no doubt my pride & joy
just simply knowing I am loved
by my precious little boy

so small but strong
Right from the very start
his hyperness & ability
are coming from his heart

so many things are different
my life is rearranged
my perfect way of knowing
life will change

LIFE

we are so destructive
rather poor or full of wealth
we seem to look at dollar signs
more than we do our health

we lose sight of what's important
refusing to ever see
the life that we are living
is our own Reality

we try to pass the blame
for the faults that we might live
never asking ourselves (did we)
give all have to give

so easy to blame another
for what we did or didn't do
it's just a part of life
and Reality so true

I think we should be satisfied
with the love with in our heart
because we can't see where we're heading
if we don't know where to start

lonely alone

meaningless words
for all to see
there shallow & worthless
to all but me

nobody knows
just what I feel
& only me
would know that it's real

I except all comments
good & bad
for the stories I tell
of the life I had

no doubt I will make it
I still have my home
I've learned to live with
lonely alone

heartfelt expressions
for all to see
I am a poet
with a destiny

Love in the first degree

is there a place in her heart
that only she can see
does it tell her that she really is
coming back to me

I am so far from perfect
& I really just don't know
is she coming back to me
or is she letting go

Reality has set in
it has me pinned to the floor
I feel she's not coming back
to me anymore

there isn't any future
or any sign of life
my home is now my prison
without my wife

there aren't any smiles
for anyone to see
I'm guilty & imprisoned for
love in the first degree

love Roy

give them time
they will forget
& have a life
with no regret

I was so wrong
I now can see
a happy life
does not need me

I make everyone sad
that comes in my life
if you have a doubt
just ask my wife

the key to their smiles
is staying away
there happiness gets better
everyday

she will find what she needs
with somebody else
her heart will no longer
be on a shelf

I love you all
& it is clear
I must do this
for the ones so dear

I won't hurt you no more
this way you know it
goodbye & I love you
from the hot shot poet

Marriage

after three marriages
not one seem to see
that my entire life
were my kids & me

nothing else matters
not my future or wife
my kids are my all
they are my life

I feel it's the way
God wanted it to be
& if for some reason I'm wrong
then why is he looking at me

he tells me to do
what I feel is right
so this is my motive
every day & night

I do believe he speaks
directly to me
he shows me the way
of what I need to be

so trust in this
if he speaks your name
just open your heart
& he will do the same

Mastering affection

in the glimmer of affection
we always seem to gloat
but if you don't remember how
then you should be taking notes

the gloating just comes natural
for everything that lives
but to master the affection
you must give all you can give

to simply win affection
is easier said than done
each person has the feelings
that are meant for only one

sometimes we may try to hard
wondering what we're doing wrong
but if it is meant to be
it will surely come along

there is a time & place for everything
and a way it should be done
so stop thinking your alone
because you're not the only one

for patience is a virtue
& a friend of mine
so if your seeking someone's affection
then simply give it time

maybe you should know

I know that I love you
that is a fact
I will spend all my life
just showing you that

your everything I ever wanted
and all I can see
as pure as the wind
and the purest part of me

every single breath I take
and everything I do
is all a part of me
loving only, you

I've never known a love like this
anytime of my life
you are the perfect beauty
and my precious wife

I cannot write for anyone
the way I write for you
because every time I look
I see my dreams coming true

Meaningless words

I could write a poem
in five minutes' flat
but there would be no motive
of this or that

there would be no feelings
at least none of mine
no imagination at all
in one single line

creating the Rhymes
is easy to do
but with no feeling inside
the words won't be true

they'd only be words
or quotes with fear
they won't make a smile
or create a tear

there would be no meaning
just want to be quotes
just meaningless rhymes
or a paperless note

well we all know
that it is not me
the way I've always been
is the way I will be

Memories 2

sweeping up the memories
to put them in a jar
always waking up wondering
where or how you are

so close but yet so far away
it feels like a world apart
even though you are not with me
your always in my heart

if I could turn back time
back to a brighter day
I would get to hold you
& you would hear me say

your everything in life to me
nothing can take your place
the precious bond we have together
& the smile upon your face

I will not give up hope
that's something I can't do
I love & miss you very much
it's all your dad can do

Merry Christmas to all

Christmas is finally here
new years on the way
I wish you all the very best
through the holidays

may your wishes all be granted
with everything you do
that is my wish
& it's given to all of you

in the new year may you prosper
with the goals that may be set
if we don't attempt to reach them
it could be our one regret

life is full of challenges
that just require a chance
the efforts we put forward
shall assure that we enhance

the lives of our families
in everything we do
so merry Christmas & best wishes
with love to all of you

mindset

the mind it evaluates
all it feels or see's
from a very Romantic movie
to a cooling summer breeze

from the sight of a crash
your frantic on what to do
that's seeing & feeling
& it's all a part of you

knowing your very next move
it's not how it's meant to be
it's confrontation of the moment
that shows true Reality

if we always knew our next move
in this life we live
the challenge of trying new things
we'd have no new to give

so let your mind evaluate
though you laugh or you may cry
never overlook
& always wonder why

somethings might comfort you
& some you may **Regret**
but our mind controls our next move
& the way our life is set

although you may not understand
mindset in any way
but it is a part of your life
& you feel it everyday

Misery

A place I've found
That's hell to be
is locked up tight
in misery

It holds you tight
It has no fear
It has no reaction
to blood or tears

It has no patience
or time to spare
to keep it simple
It really doesn't care

It has no timing
It comes at will
All it has
is time to kill

So for free advice
Take it from me
Don't get caught up
in misery

Missing

Directly in line
of a prayer & a dream
for so long I thought was missed
at least to me it seemed

a part of my life
that had been out of reach for years
my phone Rang & I answered it
& instantly the tears

there was a Rugged voice
on the other end of the line
at first I was confused
as it took me back in time

this young man started talking
about a dream he had
he said it was time that he changed his life
& he wants to see his Dad

at a total loss for words
not Realizing why
his voice had started quivering
trying to hide it as he cried

his mother told him years ago
I didn't want to be a part
of his lonely little life
a piece missing of my heart

& all his mother told me
is your son hates you
he doesn't want to be a part
of anything you do

there are no easy answers
for why she said these things
but together now we can mend our hearts
with what the future brings

I won't bring back the past
but I will do all I can
to be a Father to my son
& be the Dad that I am

money

it must be hard
with all that class
to strut around
with your head in your a**

you act like your better
than anybody around
your flying high
with your feet on the ground

you say that your better
than everyone & me
but even a blind man
could truly see

money has made you
what you think you are
with your diamond Rings
& your overpriced car

you think money buy's all
you think dreams are made of
it might buy you fame
but it won't buy you love

so while you prance around
& do what you do
you wonder why
your dreams don't come true

money will buy you this
& might get you that
it may even own
the place you are at

but when all is done
you wonder what did I do
for the emptiness you feel
that is the real you

when the money is gone
& your feeling so bad
only then will you see
the life you had

you can't take it back
now this is true
you cut everyone down
that had less money than you

the root of all evil
has made you choke
your so embarrassed
but your also broke

don't say you're sorry
for the cruel things you said
the true colors come out
when money goes to your head

must know

there's a few things that I'm hopeful for
& a few things that are true
they are always right beside me
 no matter what I do

the one thing that I'm hopeful for
& hope you see the light
& give our hearts the chance
to make our love right

the response must be answered
with a yes or a no
the only way I can determine
which way my heart will go

the answer is not important
but to determine what you feel
I deserve to know what it is
so the answer must be real

I don't want any games
if you do have someone else
tell it like it is
I have the perfect shelf

Hearts on fire

Beneath the flame
& beyond desire
One touch from you
& my hearts on fire

The perfect angel
So full of love
Without a doubt
What dreams are made of

You opened the door
& turned on the lights
You pulled me close
& held me tight

You filled me with love
Dignity & pride
& you promised to always
Stand by my side

I've never known love
So warm to the touch
My hearts on fire
& I love you so much

Five precious gifts

Look at what we've done
We've brought into this world
One handsome boy
& four precious girls

I've never been much for presents
Not that I recall
But the five you have given me
Are the greatest gifts of all

They cling to one another
As family members should
& I know they'd be here with me
If there were a way, they could

Jason, Amanda & Julie
Aron & Ariel
Their the same but so different
With their own story to tell

This is to let them know
no matter what we do
mommy & daddy's love is there
& always very true

my Christmas

Christmas time is coming
it's not so far away
I'm all the life that I will see
here on Christmas day

no sneaky little children
trying hard to see
who's the person putting gifts
underneath the tree

I wish them all the best
& Mommy you too
I hope you find what you seek
and all your dreams come true

I did my part to make your life
as blue as it could be
and I do deserve everything
that's happening to me

I can't take back my past
to this there is no doubt
after 10 years you have found
your own way out

so may life grant you everything
your heart's dreaming of
one day you will find it
& you will be in love

my every dream

you're all that I think about
every night & day
the only woman in the world
that takes my breath away

the only one that inspires me
in anything I do
knowing I can do anything
as long as I have you

our love was not by chance
to this there's no debate
from the day I first saw you
it's all been fate

every dream I want
to ever see come true
& everything I wish for
is all surrounding you

everything I've ever wanted
in all parts of my life
please don't stop loving me
or being my wife

My poetry

I use to think my mind controlled
all within my sight
but the fact is that my heart
controls everything, I write

all though the thoughts are in my mind
it's where the poem starts
but to satisfy what I look for
it must Run through my heart

no matter if its happy thoughts
or even if it's sad
they seem to bring out good
they also bring out bad

the words they just appear
in the night & in the day
they seem to bring out everything
I truly want to say

I do my best to write them
so everyone can see
the inspiration of my heart
creates my poetry

my reply

I read a comment on another site
the one about 'Florida' home
I was very disturbed by the comment he left
so I responded with thoughts of my own

his comment was simple "Florida is for Jews"
I detest those kind of remarks
so I wrote him my response
he created an angry spark

dear Mr. Idiot
how are you today?
I hope that it is miserable
for what you had to say

there is no prejudice in my life
at any given time
Race, creed or color
is not a problem of mine

so if you read more of my poetry
I will give this advice to you
another racist remark that I happen to find
This is what I will do

most sites will not tolerate
Remarks that do offend
if another comes through my promise to you
your access to that site will end

we come on these sites simply to say
what we feel from our hearts with in
then you show up with a dumb remark
that's where my anger begins

do you notice there are no curse words
though I have plenty to say
but I must hold respect for the true poets
who read my work everyday

so if you see my name on a poem
the best advice for you
just pass it by let me tell you why
it's the best thing you can do

My way

another beautiful day
kicked in the butt
it's still pretty early
& the door just shut

she's mad once again
I have no clue why
I won't find the answer
because I won't even try

I've dealt with this mess
for too many years
now I'm seeing my children
with angry tears

I will not tolerate
nothing hurting my kids
not even their feelings
the way my dad did

no matter what anyone thinks
they are my life
I'd give up my breath
even my wife

I'd be dead without them
this is a fact
they must always know
I've got their back

that is my job
that's what I do
I show my kids
a love that is true

it never goes away
it's forever more
I love my children
it's what my forever is for

My words

I am a poet
let it be known
the words that I write
in my heart have grown

I put them together
to build rhymes I choose
some are of winning
& some to lose

it's my personal way
to make the world look bright
it's what I do best
with all my might

along with my words
you will sometimes see
laughter & smiles
instead of tragedy

my goal is to split
with nothing to hide
the good times & bad
the love & the pride

Myth of Love

they say love
is like the driven snow
well I think it's more
like mistletoe

it wraps around
& consumes its place
it continues to grow
in any given space

I've even heard said
of a gravitational pull
I don't know about you
but to me that's bull

the only gravity I know of
holds us on the ground
if it weren't for that
we could all float around

but I do think love is awesome
so many lessons we have learned
from being as lucky as can be
to really getting burned

even I have been there
many times throughout the years
I feel it's the embarrassment
that makes us shed the tears

well also because it's painful
so very deep inside
it can consume your every move
& always messes with your pride

so at least remember this
if your ignoring everything else
no matter what your love life is
always be yourself

Names

these names they chose for me
to me they mean the same
from 'Legendary Poet'
to 'Poet Hall of Fame'

'Fan Favorite' is okay
'Published Poet' I like too
'Poets friend 'I find Reasonable
it's what we Poet's do

'Hall of Fame' I'm not sure of
'Editor' is sure not me
but 'Critic for the Poetry'
we all have to be

now 'Poetry Promoter'
I could never do
for your words are always special
when they come from you

just simple little phrases
to help connect a Rhyme
it only takes ambition
& a little bit of time

No Fear

I'm not afraid of dying
I'm not afraid to lose
I'm not afraid of love
it's the thought of being used

it seems to come to mind
when someone gets inside my heart
so I've stored it in a box
so it won't get torn apart

this box is made of steal
with cotton deep inside
so if my heart's to bleed
it won't leak away my pride

storing all emotion's
& hiding them so well
they have a story of their own
but they refuse to tell

of many heart disasters'
most eye's will never see
the life inside this poet
or the poet inside of me

no more waiting for daddy

we've been through some hardships
with agonizing pain
I never thought I'd hear
your voice again

I've always taught you to speak your mind
you did & what did it do
not paying attention to my girl
I lost contact with you

you were only nine
you tried to talk to me
I know I took it the wrong way
that much I can see

if I could take back all the hurtful words
I'd take them back today
I read your poem from your heart so true
these words you had to say

called daddy I'll wait for you
I can say one thing for sure
I promise you will have
to wait no more

Braveheart

you are my little "Braveheart"
the name that you chose
to show your skill through your words
so everybody knows

I'm proud of you my daughter
& I love you so much
daddy would give all he has
his life & such

just to show
that my love is true
there's nothing at all
that I wouldn't do

so please believe me
when I say
my love for you
is here to stay

I love you Ariel Leann Andrews
always your dad The hot shot poet

nobody but me

this is what I call my downtime
my internet is down
but still I choose to write
while nobody makes a sound

I seem to find enjoyment
creating simple Rhymes
sharing thoughts about everything
& any place & time

a simple stress Reducer
at least it is for me
it tends to take the edge off
just writing poetry

I'll probably never be as perfect
as I wish I could
& my spelling won't always be Right
like I know they should

it is nobody's fault
no one to blame but me
it's the simple way I live my life
& how I choose to be

one wing in the fire

(my kids believe this is me)

have you ever heard a song
to me it's strong desire
it's 'an angel with no halo
& one wing in the fire

my kids say that it fits
with everything I do
I know that I am blessed
to have a love this strong & true

they never seem to look at
the defaults of my past
they only see the good things
the one's they know will last

they say anyone can be a father
& it's very hard to be a dad
my heart is always open
rather they've been good or bad

they are my precious angels
no matter what they do
my love is unconditional
so strong & very true

with all of my devotion
I really do admire
I'm an angel with no halo
& one wing in the fire

only for my son

the only tears that I have
are only for my son
but I need to keep my head up high
& do what must be done

this is the hardest thing
that my life has ever seen
he's the reason that I walk & talk
& all that's in between

I can't afford a lawyer
so all that I can do
is hope that god hears me
& knows I'm being true

I would do anything
to find the help I need
to be reunited with my son
so my heart no longer bleeds

determination drives me
to do what must be done
I'm broke & it's hard
but I'm fighting for my son

only in dreams

Things that show up
 only in dreams
the more you see them
the realer they seem

Rather brutal & scary
or Romantically based
Dreams have a reason
for how they are placed

their kind of a kickback
of things on your mind
I think you could see them
even if you were blind

They say dreams have meanings
but no one knows what
Rather true or False
It's the way we were taught

some seem so real
They can make you scream
just always Remember
They're only a dream

only you can make a difference

Boxed up emotion's
covering up your pride
you might think it's a secret
but it really cannot hide

floating around inside of you
causing anger everywhere
some people just can't see it
& others just don't care

it consumes every piece of you
it can leave you all alone
it can destroy a perfect family
& the house you call a home

it can make you very bitter
even towards the one's you love
if you do not learn to let it go
it's what your life will be made of

so try to make a difference
one that makes you smile
it might stay threw eternity
or just a little while

the object of this poem
is to simply make a plan
because if anyone can make a difference
it's simple "you can"

open your eye's

(written for a friend in need of a wakeup call)

you'd fallow him through anything
through tragedy & pain
to hope he takes you seriously
& not take your words in vein

you surrender all that you believe
to show him that it's real
overlooking the most important part
just how he made you feel

he criticizes without reason
not caring what he's done
the hurt is not within him
you're the only one

your feelings they are radical
like an animal going wild
but your heart is like a toy
& to him you are a child

he plays with your emotion's
no matter what you do
he could care less what you're feeling
because it's only hurting you

outlined

there is one thing in life
that is no surprise to me
how I so simply spend my time
writing true life poetry

it use to be so difficult
to find what would inspire
but the answer was so simple
it's what the heart would Require

from every lesson learned
to losing what you love
& everything that's natural
what life is all made of

from living in a dream
to the son I love so much
every single thing I cared about
& every single touch

so many different feelings
in everything I see
no matter how sad it is
it is reality

everything I've longed for
& everything I do
it's all part of my dreams
& my dreams coming true

it is no longer my wife
or what she has took
I'm placing my devotion
in writing a book

Pieces

sweeping up the pieces
of what life use to be
searching for that someone
who might believe in me

I know I must start over
starting here & now
the only problem is
I really don't know how

how to make companionship
I've been secluded for so long
I thought by staying to myself
I could never go wrong

I never learned to mingle
or go out on a date
it seems that what I didn't do
wants to be my fate

but I have determination
what has to be will be
I'll just go on with my life
& maybe I will see

there is A lady somewhere
waiting for a special day
they will find that certain someone
to make their worries go away

everybody wants to smile
& be happy with their love
its what life is all about
what dreams are all made of

Persistence

as silent as a picture
important in my life
lying there so peacefully
this would be my wife

I tiptoe through the house
so I don't disturb her dreams
if you've ever done this
then you know what I mean

I do hope that she knows
that I love her very much
after 9 years of marriage
I still admire her touch

against everybody's thought's
& their every little doubt
we've shown them we can make it
& how all things work out

persistence is the answer
determined in what we do
just proves if you want it
your dreams can all come true

Pictures don't lie

all I have are pictures
such a tragedy
the best part about pictures
is they won't lie to me

there now the biggest part of me
& always sincere
they do not hurt me with words
what they think I want to hear

they do not get my hopes up
not in any given way
they just reflect on memories
of a better day

I know that they will be there
for the rest of my life
I no longer have my family
& I no longer have a wife

it's clear now she's not coming back
it wasn't hard to see
there are no more tomorrows
she is through with me

Poems & Reality

I get a lot of comments
on the poetry I write
sometimes they make no since at all
just to my inner sight

some have made folks furious
some have filled folk's hearts with cheer
now & then I write a funny one
& some that fill your eye's with tears

this is my obsession
what I simply love to do
just to get a small Reaction
from people just like you

I've been cut down so many times
for writing what I feel
Rather critics want to believe or not
they come from life so Real

I simply do not make up stories
& I refuse to tell a lie
my Poems must be real life
not even I can answer why

Poetry

anything imaginable
anything at all
just any little story
my mind can recall

it doesn't matter sweet or sad
whatever it may be
it is how we create the heart felt
in our poetry

so I think about my history
fresh out of my mind
I don't skip the vital pages
of any day or time

it's sort of like an Essay
you are writing with a pen
a beginning & a middle
then a perfect stories end

I'm talking to myself
& answering too
it is strangely defined
but this is what I do

I think of something from my past
or what I might have seen
create the verses one by one
to say just what I mean

I know there far from perfect
but that's alright with me
they are truth beyond a doubt
of only what I see

imagination is everything
the heart wants to see
those are the main ingredients
in my poetry

the logic in my words
I try to make where all can see
they are not just me mumbling
but they are Reality

power with in

waking up in paradise
is as mythical as can be
it's kind of like running blindfolded
& slamming into a tree

when you take your blindfold off
you'll wonder where your thought's were at
you might feel your heads a baseball
& someone else has swung the bat

the moral of my story
is simple but so true
paradise is only in our minds
it's different from me to you

if we only close our eye's
we can be what we desire
it's what cerate's our dream world
it can push us to inspire

to be the best at anything
you only need a goal
if you're not to blind to see it
it is within your soul

pride & joy

(this is my world)

he is the greatest gift
that god has given to me
he is my very future
& all my life will be

he wakes up every morning
comes straight to find his dad
this bond is so untouchable
the best we've ever had

he says he just don't understand
why mommy just won't see
he is where he belongs
where he is meant to be

he says read this to me
he loves just what I do
he says daddy I will write poetry
just like you

I am truly blessed
with my baby boy
he's the reason I do everything
my precious pride & joy

pure love

one thing that I think about
is my wife so mad at me
I feel like she is killing
what I hoped my life would be

usually when we make mistakes
we somehow find a chance
to turn our life back
to when we both felt romance

I don't care what has happened
you are still my wife
you're the only one I want to see
for the rest of my life

I love you very much
you are reality
this problem is a speedbump
& what has to be will be

please don't throw our love away
it's everything I know
without you in my life
my life has nowhere to go

Rambling on

always out fixing things
to keep my life on track
sometimes it's overwhelming
when there back to back

there's never a dull moment
in this life I live
but still you will find me
giving all I have to give

no matter what the problem is
I'm sure I've seen it all
always picking up the pieces
& always on the ball

to sit down & relax
I never have the time
but when I have a free moment
I'm always making Rhymes

my life stays in the fast lane
but I like it that a way
it's a part of being me
& that's all I have to say

Reality Dreamer

a special kind of woman
my eyes have yet to see
is simply one who understands
& believes in me

one who doesn't question
every single thing I do
but knows there is a reason
& my intentions are so true

one who finds the faith in me
& knows I'm true to only one
& she knows that things are meant to be
the way that things are done

when I find these simple things
I'll know I found my fate
& with that I'll show the truest love
I will not hesitate

maybe I've always had these things
with a lady on my mind
her impression is so perfect
& I cannot leave behind

Rhyme

I can do this all day long
every day of the week
& if I didn't have a family
I'd never have to speak

I could tell a story
that truly would be mine
I can write about anything
& anyplace or time

if a pictures worth a thousand words
a thought should be too
for it can always paint a picture
of the many things we do

don't look a gift horse in the mouth
now that I do find strange
hopefully you're a Vet.
or maybe your deranged

kill two birds with one stone
now that I'd have to see
but killing birds is not my style
so I will just let that one be

even with these crazy sayings
they paint a picture in your mind
but there not about the picture
they are about the Rhyme

sanity & dreams

I dreamed I was standing
in a mythical place we seem to call cloud nine
then suddenly the cloud was gone
but I was left behind

I hope that wasn't my paradise
because it left me standing still
with no one to speak to but myself
I hope this isn't free will

If it is it's turn around
it's backed me in a hole
it tries to take all that I am
but it cannot touch my soul

it could offer me the riches of any man
it still wouldn't help them out
that part of me stays with me
it's mine without a doubt

so come on you beast of sanity
try with all your might
as long as I believe you cannot win
this I know is right

believers are winners& winners believe
this can't be taken away
it's been around before my time
& until my dying day

Searching

What will it take
What must I do
To find a love
So strong & true

To find the one
That's meant for me
My other half
my destiny

The one I see
Every night & day
The one that wants me
In every way

The one that sees
Love is not blind
The one that wont
Leave me behind

Someone who knows
what dreams are made of
Someone who knows
About true love

she's done with me

from the first time that I saw you
the day that we did meet
my only destination
was to sweep you off your feet

so precious & so innocent
you stopped the hands of time
what I've wanted all my life
wanted to be mine

we've been married now 10 years
& I am still in love
she isn't just my dream girl
she's what my dreams are all made of

she drove a thousand miles
just to be with me
to see if I could make her life
the best that it could be

my destructive heart has failed her
now she is done with me
she's moved back to her home state
to be happy & free

she doesn't want to be around
anything in my life
I suppose when she is done
she'll no longer be my wife

I wouldn't want to be around someone
who made me feel that bad
she was everything in the world
& all I ever had

she's gone

no time to regret
nobody was wrong
she made up her mind
& she was gone

she took my son
Right out of my life
no more family
& no more wife

years of struggle
protecting my son
neglecting her feelings
it can't be undone

it is much too late
for I'm sorry for that
I deserve what I'm feeling
& where I am at

she wanted to go
I have no doubt
I assume she felt
it was the only way out

I pray she is happy
where ever she goes
the life she left
for the life she chose

no bitter remarks
no missing her touch
just tell my son
I love him so much

she's not through with me

my heart says you're not through
you're not throwing me away
your simply not a quitter
not on any day

there is something in your voice
as I read you poetry
a whisper in my mind says
you're not through with me

absence makes the heart grow fonder
with every passing day
if there's a way to bring you back to me
then love will find a way

there has never been a love
to make me feel like this
I'm giving it my all
& hope I haven't missed

the only chance at the truest love
my life will ever know
I love my wife very much
& it will always show

when she reads this poem
I hope that she will see
there's something deep inside
saying she's not through with me

should

I want to take her breath away
so she will know just what I see
when she looks into my eye's
& her heart is touching me

nobody but my wife
can make me feel like this
I'm amazed by the simple things
the ones I truly miss

if I have the chance
to ever make this right
A day will never pass
I'm not holding her so tight

I didn't see just what I had
until it was gone
I went from waking up with life
to waking up alone

I wish upon all falling stars
that somehow I could see
my only love & laughter
is coming home to me

simple faith

it started with a vision
so deep in the night
telling me have faith
everything will be alright

the voice said it saw me
as sad as I can get
then it said I can't give up
for it's not over yet

everything will fall in place
as long as I believe
all things happen for a Reason
& your son you will Retrieve

enduring pain and loneliness
what life is all about
but to honestly find happiness
you must believe without a doubt

so I put my faith in his hands
everywhere I go
it makes my life possible
now it's time for it to show

simple little Rhymes

more than just a bunch of words
thrown together to make a page
more trying than any actor
with their first time on a stage

our words may be meaningless
to readers everywhere
but it is our way of reaching out
our priceless way to share

our daily life activities
of whatever we're going through
most would say they've heard it all
but to the writer it is new

it is our way of making contact
when realities arise
creating something out of nothing
right before your eye's

most don't seem to understand
the words we try to say
but most poets understand perfectly
this is just our way

this is our little world
to most it's out of time
but we tell the stories of ourselves
with simple little rhymes

simply from the heart

they ask me if I can make
folks feel what I feel
I really don't know
but I know it is real

to understand my poetry
or even be able to see
you must understand
the reality of me

I am a simple man
it's all I can do
to put my words together
& make them visible to you

if you do not understand them
or don't know where to start
then maybe your just reading
& not reading from the heart

anything worth reading
is worth reading all the way
if your heart gets involved
you'll understand what I say

Simply understanding

some people know the answers
the things you need to hear
they seem to know just what to say
to fill you up with cheer

just simple little words
no one else has said
puts all things in respective
& not just in your head

what I need to say is thank you
as I await the day to end
your words were out of kindness
& spoken like a friend

I do wish there were more like you
it would open people's eye's
giving them the strength they need
so they might realize

sometime life is tricky
but mostly for the best
we follow feelings everywhere
with hopes our heart can pass the test

so thank you very much
you brought my inspiration back
now I think with my persistence
I'll get me back on track

this is how I know to thank you
I hope my words will show it
you lit a candle to brighten up
the hot shot poet

sometimes we write just to write

in the heart of a man
who always does his best
& the mind of this man
that never seems to Rest

I can Rest forever
after I am dead
that is my philosophy
that courses through my head

I am not a movie star
I'm barely anything
so I do my best with my words
to see what smiles I'll bring

but everyone is different
in the simplest of ways
one will say they can Relate
& others simply say

your poem has no meaning
so they do not understand
how to find the feeling
in the words of this man

If you can **Read,** it with your eye's
then try to **Read** it with your heart
If you truly want to understand
then this is where you start

to see beyond the words
of the verses that you read
some may fill your heart with love
or just simply fill a need

for some it won't do anything
but boggle up the mind
one of the many differences
of these days & times

sometimes

no matter what I do
no matter what it takes
I always seem to find
a way to make mistakes

in time to mess up anything
my heart would try to do
my pride would make a heart
& my mind would paint it blue

an unsuccessful thing to do
straight from the start
it's a lonely way to be
when you want to win a heart

anything I ever do
on any day or night
shows anything that I do
is worth doing right

just simple little lines
to show just what I see
we do not have to want it
but sometimes it must be

still in love

every time you touch me
with just your fingertips
it never takes me very long
to be looking for your lips

the softest of all kisses
that I have ever seen
you are the Romantic girl
I find in all my dreams

everything about you
every little touch
nobody can replace
that's why I need you so much

everything you stand for
is everything I miss
it's everything in my dreams
like loves first kiss

you have a way about you
when I look into your eye's
do you really know
or even realize

everything about you
is what my dreams are all made of
there is no doubt about it
I'm still in love

still missing you

here I am again
up again by 2
it seems to always happen
because I'm always missing you

it didn't take me long to realize
what I need in my life
it's no more than my children
& my precious wife

they are what I'm living for
my heart says there's a way
to show you what we're missing
what words could never say

I need to feel the love again
that went so far away
the love my life is all about
it is my night & day

my heart hopes for 3 words
as we're talking on the phone
maybe soon you'll say
I'm coming home

survival of the heart

I am contemplating
trying hard to see
what it is your thinking
that makes you mad at me

I do my best to show my love
& bring a smile around
& no matter what I try
you always bring me down

maybe you were right
for leaving from the start
we were alone together
just like we are apart

I want so bad to fix this
but it can't be done alone
trying to bring us back together
I feel I'm on my own

my heart can break no more
it's shattered all apart
so if you think we have a chance
you'll have to save my heart

take a chance

I want to take your breath away
with a very tender touch
do all the little things
that use to mean so much

to gently touch your lips
& say that I love you
& hold you so close to me
the way you want me to

I truly need to hold you
& say forever more
I know that I have never been
in love like this before

I know I've made a mess of things
trying to be in your life
but I truly can't help it
I love you & my wife

I can see now without you
is as lonely as can be
I pray that you will take a chance
& come back to me

to be the man I use to be
that set your world on fire
do all the things you love
& all that you desire

the challenge

you have made a challenge
and aimed it at my heart
to see if you took all my love
if my life would fall apart

well I have to say you did it
you showed your dignity
your friends & your family
know you have no use for me

it was hard for me to face it
but reality set in
my families gone forever
their new smiles will begin

no happiness beyond these walls
no laughter in the wind
10 years was her final run
now she's forcing it to end

so goodbye & good luck
with everything you do
just give it time you will unwind
& your dreams will all come true

The hardest thing I'll ever do is Telling you goodbye

I'm writing this to my daughters
it is the best that I can do
these lies you told are haunting me
& I pray there haunting you

you all know I've done nothing
except try to be a dad
but It seems it wasn't good enough
& I gave it all I had

I will always love you
you all know this is true
so for the sake of my sanity
here's what I've got to do

I will no longer do this
I've tried with all my might
now I'll give what you seem to want
it's my parental rights

I do not feel you need me
in your lives anymore
I feel this will make you happy
& this is what it's for

I wish you all the best
that life can truly give
I pray that you find happiness
in the life you chose to live

you three girls have torn my heart out
what more can I say
the cruel things you have lied about
will never go away

you will never have to see me
as of right now I am gone
I will not be in your life
I'm leaving you alone

for over 17 years I've fought for you
& always done what's right
so for you three & your mother
as of now I'm out of sight

the hunt

to put away the memories
that tore my world apart
not knowing what to do
or how to find my heart

I've searched for it everywhere
in my truck & on the floor
it seems I have lost track of it
that much is for sure

confusion has devoured me
I am so very lost
this is the price I'm paying
the pain is the cost

searching for the help I need
to bring my son home
he says that without me
he feels so all alone

I know that I must find a way
to help my baby see
that all will be alright
& he will be back with me

he is my everything
in everything I've done
he's the reason I won't quit
he truly is my son

last poem on her

well I finally got my answer
not what I hoped it would be
dissolution of marriage
means she is through with me

she's trying to say it's not a divorce
but I have seen it twice
it's not at all what I hoped for
& in no way is it nice

I was convinced she was coming back
but in all reality
all she said was she doesn't know
now the truth will set her free

I got what I deserve
living all alone
she is through with me
she's not coming home

this is my last poem
there is nothing to inspire
the heartfelt poetry
now must be retired

the life of a poet

were different from all the rest
not long after we're born
we can find a recipe
for any heart that's torn

we are a family of the gifted
& we want all to see
the lives that we live
through our poetry

we are no different
than anyone of you
we've just trained our thoughts
for doing what we do

to find the word unspoken
in every single line
to find another meaning
in just a little time

we always do our best
we hope our words will show it
the pure & simple life
of any kind of poet

the little boy blues

little boy, little boy
glowing with his pride
he knows he is my world
& my arms are opened wide

he wants to be like daddy
I'm unsure what he can see
the trust & devotion
he gives to only me

a heart so very fragile
so pure & full of love
I wonder if he knows
he's what my dreams are all made of

I cherish every moment
of the life we live
our bond is so untouchable
giving all we have to give

the direction of my words
& everything I do
there aimed at the happiness
in the little boy blues

the little things

I hear your voice calling me
no matter what I do
it helps me to understand
why I'm so in love with you

I miss those little fingertips
& the perfect way they touch
there are so many little things
that truly mean so much

we use to hold each other
my God I miss those days
I know that we can bring it back
& this time it will stay

on Saturday we'd go out
flea marketing & stuff
no doubt I was too dumb to see
it just was not enough

there is no one
could ever take your place
Right now I hold this picture
just to touch your face

the one thing

no shoulder to cry on
no whisper I love you
trying my best to figure out
just what I'm going through

I hear her voice everywhere
calling out to me
without her I have nothing
she is my destiny

she's everything I've ever wanted
to have in my life
she's done the best she could by me
such a precious wife

she is no doubt my Angel
the woman that I adore
I'll do anything she ask me too
to show my love is pure

maybe someday I'll find a way
to make her proud of me
she will never again wonder
what the beauty is I see

this poem is all about her
she simply is my world
to the one that I speak about
you're a very precious girl

The Scam

there are three kinds of people
the good & bad
then the one's that will take
everything you have

some people can't see
what's before there eye's
they lose everything
before they realize

it is just a front
they act so nice
they are quick minded & smart
so don't think twice

they appear to be something
that your wanting to see
if they seem to good
then take it from me

too good to be true
in their own little way
they seem to know
what you want them to say

whatever it takes
to win your trust
they do what they do
because they must

they feed on compassion
like nothing you've known
then before your eye's
all you have is gone

but don't blame your self
although you can
it's how they live
looking for the next scam

the treasure of advise

in honor of devotion
to the love my heart can see
the one who's brought me happiness
& gave me dignity

sent to me from heaven
my angel in disguise
that's all I see each time I look
so deeply in her eye's

soft spoken with each word
so gentle with her touch
it's no surprise I've found the one
I truly love so much

so if you ever find
a love you feel is true
take some advice from me
& the way that you should do

show her that you love her
she must always know you care
if you can do these simple things
you'll always have a love to share

The way I see

we spend our whole life planning
the things we want to do
but so many of us fail
& our dreams do not come true

we turn to our resources
to build another dream
we've lost our expectations
or at least that's what it seems

we try not to get discouraged
in this game we're forced to play
the game is called reality
& it changes everyday

you pick up all your pieces
then you put them in a row
but the game is over half way through
before you even know

by the time that we understand
the real game we call life
it seems to cut us deeper
than any kind of knife

this is just my opinion
each has their own to see
so rather mine is right or wrong
it still belongs to me

the way it is

there is a strong desire
in every given way
a dependency of writing
to show what I have to say

I will not write a letter
that is just not me
I send my message in the way
of homemade poetry

when I attempt to write a letter
it never comes out right
my words just seem to twist around
& somehow I'll lose sight

sight of what I meant to say
just seems to fall apart
when I reread it never comes out
like I feel it in my heart

I must stay true to my heart
in every single line
it makes it simple for me
as long as something rhymes

it may be wrong but it is
the way I've taught myself
what you feel should not be kicked around
or stock piled on a shelf

sometimes it's the smallest things
that make the most desire
like simple words that are not heard
they really can inspire

the weaker sex

I want to tell a secret
to every one of you
do you know what a man will do
to prove his love is true

he'll swallow his pride
admit when he is wrong
he'll do what he must do
to bring you back home

no doubt we are the weaker ones
our minds will go astray
we don't see what we've done
until our love is gone away

then it won't take very long
we know it's time to find
a way to fix this problem
before we run out of time

I tell you from experience
as I try to fix my heart
I'll do all the things I didn't do
so my life won't fall apart

there may be little meaning
but to make it very clear
I'll do what's right to Reunite
with the family that's so dear

things in life

you are the half
that makes me whole
the key to my heart
the door to my soul

the window of life
that I look through
& all I can see
is nothing but you

the love that I carry
so deep inside
the only cure
for wounded pride

the air that I breath
the needing your touch
is there any wonder
why I love you so much

I am far from perfect
but I try my best
to do things right
& pass the test

the test that life
has issued to me
my response will determine
just what will be

what will be in this life
what makes me thrive
I will give it my all
as long as I am alive

this little world

it's a lonely place without you
everywhere I go
the pain inside is trying me
I think everybody knows

this little world I live in
it now just seems so sad
it's taking all my energy
& all the love I have

if I had another chance
this is what I see
my family coming home
just to be with me

no misunderstandings
give that word a rest
it's time we learned to talk
& simply do our best

they are my inspiration
in all I try to do
I want to show forever
this love so true

Through a husband's eye's

if the sky was not blue
or I lived a different life
I might be able to say
I do not love my wife

but the fact of the matter is
through arguments & such
she's the reason I am here
& I love her very much

the reason that I have
to hold my head up high
she is always looking out for me
& I have to wonder why

through all the hell I put her through
she's always standing by my side
& when life tries to destroy me
her arms are opened wide

when life drops me to my knees
no matter where or when
she always seems to be there
to stand me up again

this goes out to all the husbands
unsure of the life they live
unless you want your world to fall apart
give all the love you have to give

but if you are unsure
then you can hesitate
& in the blinking of an eye
you'll find that your too late

to be a friend

a friend is a person
that right from the start
you feel confident
to pour out your heart

things you've kept buried
so deep inside
you feel you will bust
if you continue to hide

if you trust this friend
then right from the start
you will feel secure
to pour out your heart

with things that have haunted you
through most of your life
have pierced your soul
like a very sharp knife

but when a friend is true
they will do their best
to create a path
so you heart can rest

they can't take away
the hurt inside
but through showing compassion
to restore your pride

to unlock the cage
where you store your heart
to release the rage
that tore you apart

so with these words
the message I send
I am truly honored
to be your friend

to be a man

A man is incredible
his life will Rearrange
just to convince
somebody he will change

sometimes in desperation
he thinks he truly can
but I tell you from experience
that a man is just a man

the weaker of the sex
a fact that's sad but true
we'll promise anything
if that's what we must do

now do not get me wrong
or what I'm speaking of
even though I know we do it
we usually do it out of love

it doesn't make us bad
or even make us wrong
like finding a description
of yourself in a song

we make ourselves what we are
to this there is no doubt
it's just a part of life
& what life is all about

(a quote "" to be a man is to make mistakes,
to be a bigger man is to admit it
when we do!!"")

to make it right

for a heart full of regret
there is only one cure
to change the way, I am
for a heart that is pure

I'm really so ashamed
I didn't see it somehow
I pushed you into where you are
& I can see it now

I don't know why I couldn't see it
all the wrong I've done
to my wife & my daughter
& even to my son

I've been in love with my wife
since she first looked in my eye's
it seems it took her leaving
to make me realize

the way I was being was hurting them
way down deep inside
I couldn't see what I was doing
until I couldn't find my pride

so Austin & Lexi
I love you all so much
you are everything in life to me
I have no life without your touch

I will turn my life around
I know just what I must do
A proud husband & a dad
with love so faithful & true

I want to make you proud of me
have your hearts so full of love
to make you want to smile
from the simple thought of

to write

I want to tell a story
that isn't hard to see
about heart felt poems
& there true Reality

they come from deep within one's self
in all amounts of lines
for me it's always easier
to stay with in my rhymes

to stay with in a story
a happening in your life
Rather it is full of happiness
or cuts just like a knife

no matter what it is
poets have their own insight
of what it takes to keep the words
in all the verses right

there's always a beginning
a middle & an end
it could be about a love
a family or a friend

no matter what you write about
your words must always show it
for me it's simply learning
for the hot shot poet

to you

you wanted to hurt me
and you succeeded
you took everything
I ever needed

you took my heart
my soul my mind
leaving the shell
of the man behind

I use to feel so needed
I thought my life was so complete
but she found herself a new life
I hope he's what she dreamed to meet

I hear her in the back ground
she's as happy as can be
I'm glad for her but knowing
she has no place for me

I hope that you found everything
that you were looking for
& the new life you are living
makes you smile forever more

totally lost

lost between the feelings
they seem to have my heart hog tied
they have trapped my emotion's
& put duct tape on my pride

they seem to have swallowed up
all I thought was me
it's one word that I can't stand
it's called jealousy

she has never had a reason to doubt me
I've been faithful all along
but her actions & her words
they tell me I'm not wrong

I will try my best to fix this
it seems to have gone too far to fix
everyday there is something new
or another little trick

like searching everything
& deleting my contact list
I tell her this is childish
but still she must persist

I have a one owner heart
& right now it belongs to me
I will fix this no matter what it takes
I guess soon we all shall see

I'd rather be a single man
then be accused of things not done
after 9 years you think she would know this
I wouldn't lie to anyone

trying to fix me

I thought I could fix anything
that my eyes could clearly see
but until now I never thought about
trying to fix me

my kids call me the fix it man
a name I'm proud to hold
I make them smile when their unhappy
at least this is what I'm told

it's always been a part of me
to simply make a smile
for anyone that would cross my path
it only took a little while

I thank god for my children
for with them I know I'm blessed
but I just cannot figure out
how I became such a mess

no matter what I try to do
there is always something not Right
no matter what it's based upon
though I try with all my might

anymore I just brush it off
to what has to be will be
it is my major imperfection
trying to fix me

trying to write a letter to you

I've never been good at letters
or knowing what to say
no matter what I try to write
a rhyme gets in the way

everything I try to write
the words do what they do
I piece them all together
& they show me loving you

through the good & bad in life
I would go anywhere
just to be with my family
& show how much I care

everything about you
from your laughter to your touch
this is what I'm missing
& I love you very much

this place I call a home
I find these words not true
my home is anywhere
I'm holding on to you

you are my lifetime princess
no matter what you do
they say home is where the heart is
& my hearts with you

Typically, me

once I've been discouraged
I never go too far
I'm wondering if you see me
when you gaze upon a star

I'm asking you this question
because I tend to see your eye's
every time that I look up
at a perfect starry sky

you'll know that I am loving
& wanting to be with you
as your talking to the stars
you'll know I'm talking to them too

I want to be a memory
that never goes away
& maybe it will bring you back
into my arms one day

you know what I am feeling
is true without a doubt
this heart belongs to you
& it will not let me out

unconditional love for you

my love is unconditional
for my precious wife
she's the answer to my prayers
& all parts of my life

she's anything & everything
I'll ever want to do
she's every single dream
that will ever come true

I don't care what has happened
I love you just the same
& no matter what it is
I blame me just the same

please tell me you love me
& that you will be coming home
& that you still believe in me
& you won't leave me alone

I'll change my life completely
whatever I must do
for I cannot see a world
without me loving you

UNCONDITIONAL

last night as I
was getting ready for bed
so many thoughts
going through my head

keeping my son
never far from sight
every day
and every night

assuring him always
I'll be by his side
it's a matter of love
and the purest of pride

the gift I've been given
with my precious son
unconditional love
that can't be undone

my world is complete
my love is so true
son you're my world
and I truly love you

UNTITLED TRUTH

I'm improving my words
I'm making my way
relying on trust
of all that I say

I condemn no one
in all that I do
but be assured
my words are true

I am the poet
of reality
I write the words
of what I see

no make believe
in what I write
true to my heart
& into your sight

the difference is simple
the words will show it
you've now been touched
by the hot shot poet

unwritten novel

you do not know my words
or what I choose to say
so how could you understand
just what I want to say

the only way that you could know
anyone can see
you must be in my heart
and be a part of me

to be within my feelings
know everything that's real
how else is it possible
to know just how I feel

well no one knows what goes on
it's only what you see
no one could just guess it
nobody but me

the wall around my heart
in everything I do
brings my words to life
so you can feel it too

unwritten words

I have a lot of friends
Poets so to speak
lost within their heart
it leaves their pride so weak

writing out every word
found within their heart
not knowing anyone can see
it's tore their world apart

lost with in emotion's
what their heart tells them to write
thinking no, one will understand
but they try with all their might

bending the foundation
of what they want to say
but I read between the lines
in every single way

so this is to my friends
with all you try to do
I read what is unwritten
& try my best for you

Voices

in the dark of night
it's always been said
if you hear voices
inside your head

pay attention to what's said
although it's not Real
it might make a difference
in how you feel

it's 4 a.m.
& I'm out of the bed
thanks to a voice
inside my head

it doesn't make since
in any way
but still I hear
what they have to say

they say nothing bad
as I'm taking a walk
it just seems to me
that it wants to talk

about all the things
throughout my life
my truck, my house,
my kids, my wife,

it only talks
about what matters to me
no crazy impressions
just Reality

so I just listen
hoping I can see
what it is there trying
to say to me

wake up call for a friend

I'm like none of the boys
that you play with their head
you'll find nothing like me
in any story you've read

you don't have the power
to turn me on
you give me sad stories
& poof your gone

my life is complicated
in ways you'll never know
so with these words
I am letting this go

I've seen enough
I'm done that's it
good luck on finding
someone who won't quit

I love you baby girl
& I'm sure that you know it
so goodbye & good luck
from the hot shot poet

I'm posting this poem
for all to see
your lies & your games
will not include me

what the eyes won't see

of all the things I always new
my life would someday see
somehow I never thought about
what is happening to me

Right at this very moment
with everything I love
with the ones I always knew
my dreams were all made of

now my dreams have past Reality
with all I've ever known
my precious spark of life
is missing from my home

the simple inspirations
of everything I've done
for the last 8 years
has revolved around my son

he is the part of life
my heart will always see
his happiness & laughter
is the very heart of me

whispers

I hear it in your voice
you're as confused as you can be
but I'm going to try to cheer you up
so maybe you will see

there is a heart in this world
that beats because of you
the undying power of love
has always helped us through

you've give me the strength
to be proud of who I am
ten years of loving you
my heart will make a stand

if there is a way on this earth
I'm going to make this right
you'll never have to wonder
if I'm going to hold you tight

I am far from perfect
but no matter what I do
my world revolves
around loving you

I am truly honored
you chose to be my wife
& I swear to you I'll show it
for the rest of my life

so to my wife & children
I love you all very much
your beautiful faces
appear on everything I touch

who is it

he was always a legend
but only in my mind
he had a rough appearance
but he was really kind

he stood up for his beliefs
no matter what the call
you could always find him
giving it his all

men would underestimate
the anger deep inside
but when they crossed that line
it was all about his pride

the man that I speak of
he has so much to tell
the reason that I know this
is I know him very well

he has so many memories
that nobody else can see
& in case you haven't figured out
this man is only me

Wonderful World

I awake every morning
& as I roll out of my bed
the most amazing thoughts
are Running through my head

what a beautiful life I have
& what a wonderful life I live
it is my inspiration
to give all that I can give

although my life is full of pain
I look past what I can feel
I seem to find the beauty
most say it is unreal

I'm living in a dream world
where all is what you see
it might not be as real to you
but it truly is to me

what a beautiful world
where your dreams are all your own
enjoy them in privacy
or you can make them known

we choose what we remember
we control what we forget
some will one day understand
& some will learn Regret

the heart & mind work as one
creating what we dream
so we will have a story
that no one has ever seen

take the ones of laughter
they might be here a while
or choose the most meaningful one's
the one's that made you smile

it is the only difference
this world can really see
it defines who we are
from who we thought we would be

The one

Understanding precious moments
and the gift of love
holding on to your happiness
that's sent from up above

leaning towards the moment
that you will finally see
the happiness you've dreamed of
the one that's meant to be

the one that's always with you
in your thoughts & on your mind
the one who holds the memories
you cannot leave behind

the one who make you tremble
with the slightest touch
the one that's in your heart
you know you love so much

only you could know
who your love is meant too be
your one & only other half
your lifelong destiny

My poems within my books
Are dating back to around 1980
To the present day which is 10/24/2015

I am proud to do what I do & honored to be able
To share my work with the world,

All over you

I'm through with hurting
I'm through with blue
I'm through with lonesome
All over you

I'm through with tear drops
& agony
I'm through with feeling
No one's wanting me

I'm through with sadness
& constant lies
It's time I wake up
& realize

I can't be sad
All over you
It just is not
The thing to do

I'll rest my heart
With someone new
Because no longer is it
All over you

ABOUT THE AUTHOR

The way to show
what I'm all about
is too pick up a pen
& write it out

Through my words
I have nothing to fear
Be it happy or sad
Or what I hold dear

Within the thoughts
Of every Rhyme
To touch a heart
will take some time

time to be caring
with words so true
& show the world
I love what I do

To share with the world
All that I see
To show everyone
This is just me

www.ingramcontent.com/pod-product-compliance
Lightning Source LLC
Chambersburg PA
CBHW051903170526
45168CB00001B/222